GLOW IN THE DARK
BOOK OF
SPACE

Published in the United States in 2002 by The Millbrook Press, Inc.,
2 Old New Milford Road, Brookfield, Connecticut 06804

Created and produced by Nicholas Harris and Claire Aston,
Orpheus Books Ltd.

Illustrated by Sebastian Quigley (Linden Artists)

Consultant: David Hawksett, Organizer of the UK Planetary Forum

Copyright © 2002 Orpheus Books Ltd.

Library of Congress Cataloging-in-Publication Data

Harris, Nicholas, 1956-
  Glow in the dark book of space / Nicholas Harris ; illustrated by Sebastian Quigley.
     p. cm.
  Includes index.
  Summary: A glow-in-the-dark introduction to astronomy, including the universe as a
whole, the stars and galaxies, and our solar system.
     ISBN 0-7613-1494-6
     1. Astronomy--Juvenile literature. 2. Glow-in-the-dark books--Specimens. [1.
Astronomy. 2. Glow-in-the-dark books. 3. Toy and movable books.] I. Quigley,
Sebastian, ill. II. Title.

QB46 .H224 2002
520--dc21   2001044106

Printed and bound in China

1 3 5 4 2

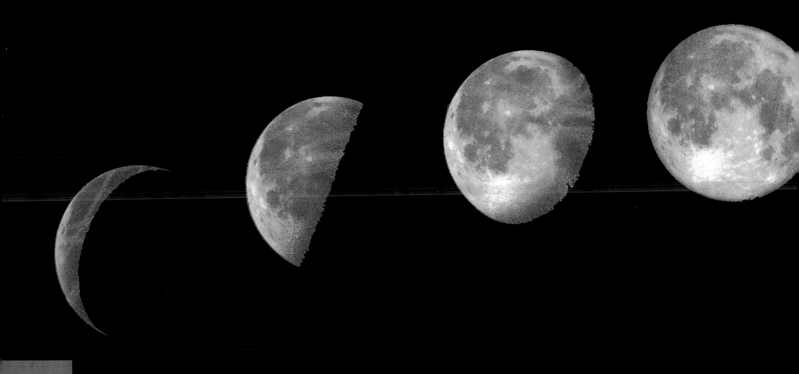

GLOW IN THE DARK
BOOK OF
SPACE

written by
Nicholas Harris

illustrated by
Sebastian Quigley

 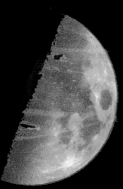 

M

The Millbrook Press

Brookfield, Connecticut

Meteors

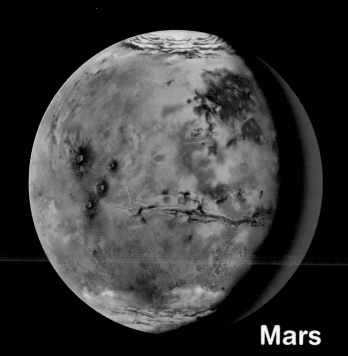

Mars

CONTENTS

WE THINK of space as the vast, dark expanse beyond our own planet Earth. The Sun's light fills the sky by day, of course, but at night other objects in space become visible: stars, the Milky Way, the Moon, shooting stars, and more. We can see these objects because they glow, either with their own light or with light reflected from the Sun. Some of those glowing objects are also glowing in the pages of this book. For the pages with special glow-in-the-dark text and illustrations, look for the pink corner squares. Hold the book open at any one of these pages under a light for twenty seconds or so, and then turn out the light.

Milky Way galaxy

ABOUT THIS BOOK

Planet

Comet

Moon

LOOK UP at the sky on a clear night. What is the brightest thing you can see? On many nights it will be the Moon. It looks so large and bright because it is our nearest neighbor in space.

The stars may look tiny, but in fact they are gigantic, thousands of times the size of Earth!

THE SKY AT NIGHT

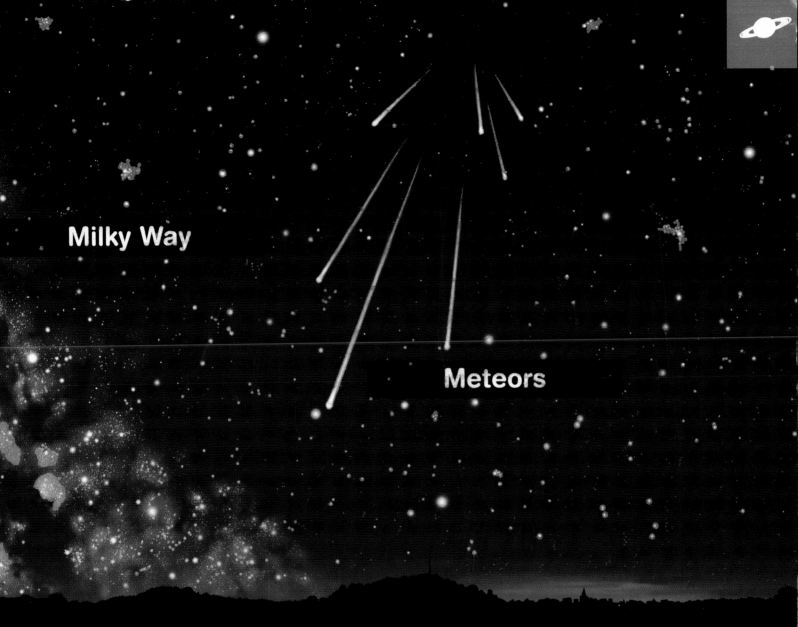

Milky Way

Meteors

All the stars we can see with the naked eye belong to the Milky Way galaxy. From Earth, one of our galaxy's spiral arms looks like a misty band across the heavens, the "milky way" from which the galaxy takes its name.

Sometimes, you may be able to catch sight of a comet hanging in the sky. Look out, too, for meteors or "shooting stars," split-second streaks of light. They are tiny fragments burning up high above Earth.

THE SUN is one of billions of stars that make up the galaxy. Like all stars, it is a giant spinning ball of very hot gas. It produces massive amounts of energy at its core.

The surface of the Sun bubbles and spits like water boiling in a pan. Huge flares and arches of glowing gas sometimes burst into space. Sunspots—dark, cooler areas—appear on the Sun's surface from time to time.

Arch

Jupiter
(to scale)

Earth
(to scale)

Flare

THE SUN

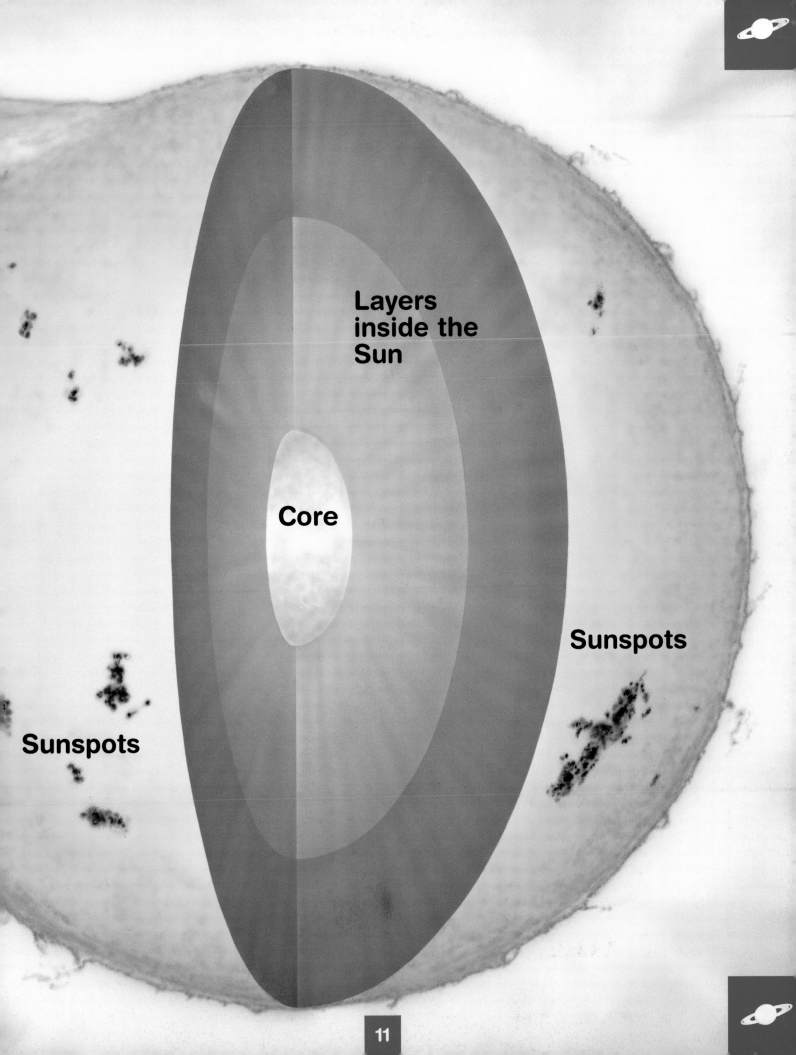

Layers
inside the
Sun

Core

Sunspots

Sunspots

THIS IS what the Milky Way would look like if we zoomed out into space and looked back down at it. It is a gigantic mass of stars. The swirling pattern the stars make is called a spiral. The galaxy has a bulge at its center. Our Sun is just one of the billions of stars in the Milky Way. It is found on one of the spiral "arms," just over halfway out from the center.

OUR GALAXY, A SPIRAL OF STARS

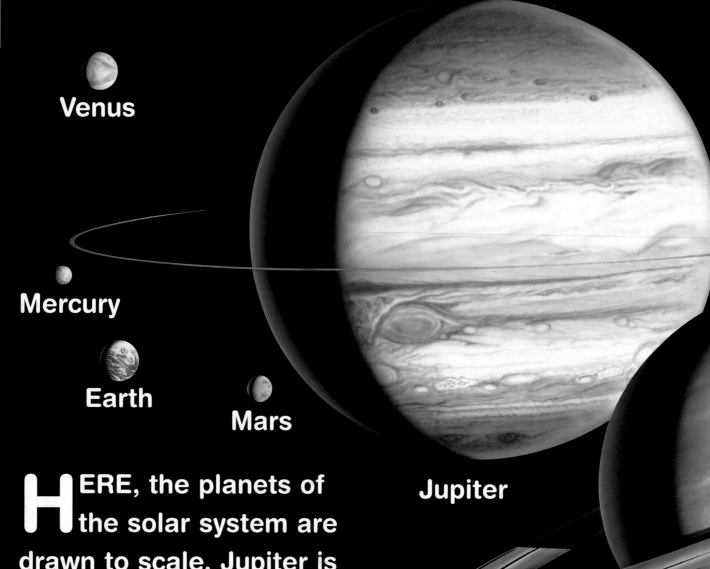

Venus

Mercury

Earth

Mars

Jupiter

HERE, the planets of the solar system are drawn to scale. Jupiter is the largest planet. It is more massive than all the others combined.

The four inner planets are Mercury, Venus, Earth, and Mars. They are made mostly of rock.

Sun
Mercury
Venus
Earth
Mars
Asteroids
Jupiter
Saturn
Uranus

The inner planets are dwarfed by four outer planets, the "gas giants" Jupiter, Saturn, Uranus, and Neptune. They are made mostly of gas. Pluto is different. A small outer planet, it is made of ice and rock.

The diagram below, also drawn to scale, shows the distance each planet lies from the Sun.

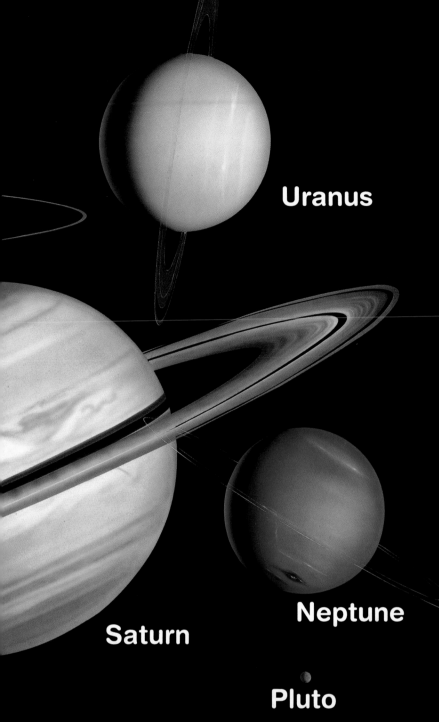

Uranus

Saturn

Neptune

Pluto

THE PLANETS TO SCALE

Pluto
(when nearest the Sun)
Neptune

Pluto
(at its furthest point from the Sun)

THE SOLAR SYSTEM consists of the Sun, its family of nine planets and their moons, comets, asteroids, meteoroids, and vast amounts of gas.

All these objects, large or small, travel around, or orbit, the Sun.

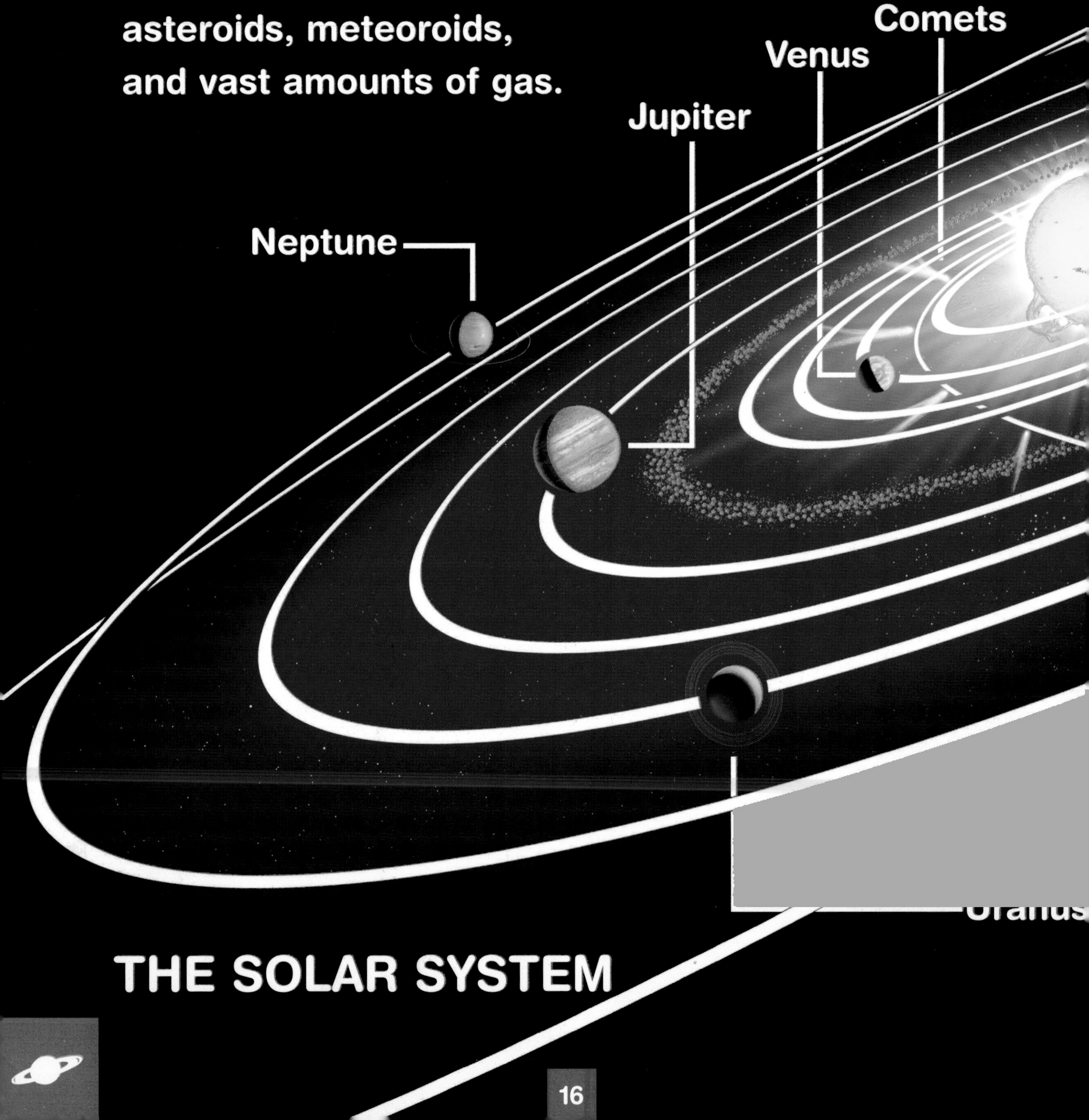

Comets

Venus

Jupiter

Neptune

THE SOLAR SYSTEM

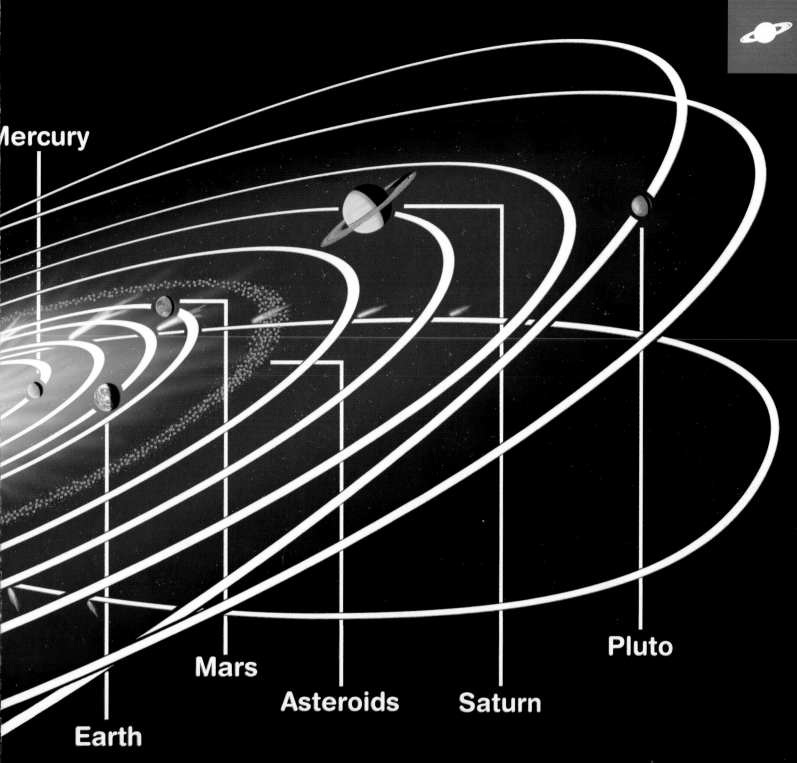

Mercury

Mars

Earth

Asteroids

Saturn

Pluto

The planets orbit the Sun in the same direction. Most of them stay on the same path. For part of its journey around the Sun,

Pluto lies inside Neptune's orbit. Many comets loop in toward the Sun from distant parts of the solar system.

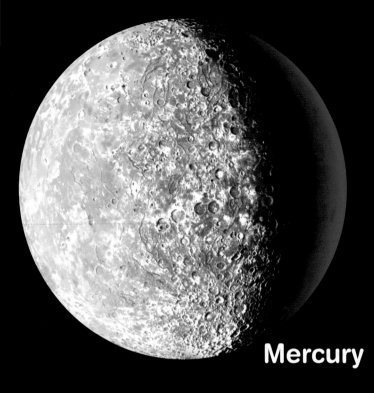

Mercury

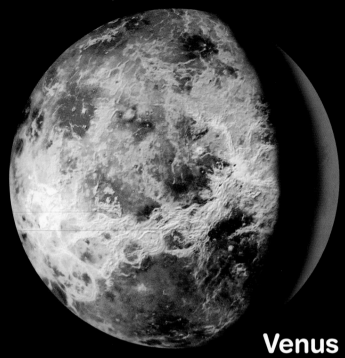

Venus

MERCURY is the nearest planet to the Sun. During the day it is extremely hot. But at night it is bitterly cold.

VENUS is covered by thick clouds of deadly acid. On its surface, the temperature is hot enough to melt lead.

EARTH is the only planet to have liquid water, vital for any life to exist. The atmosphere protects us from the Sun's harmful rays.

THE INNER PLANETS

Earth

Asteroids

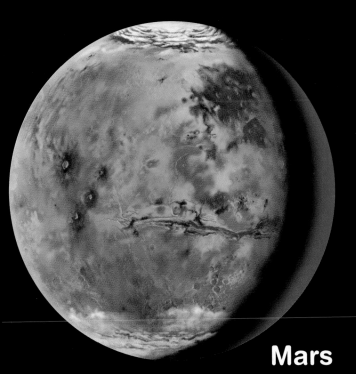

Mars

MARS is the "Red Planet," so-called because of the color of the dust that blankets its surface. Now completely barren, Mars may once have had running water. Some scientists think that there could have been life on Mars in the past. The only water on the Martian surface today is frozen at the polar ice caps.

ASTEROIDS are small blocks of rock and metal. Most are found in a belt between Mars and Jupiter. Meteoroids, fragments of asteroids, sometimes come near Earth. Comets are lumps of dust and rock frozen together. Long tails of gas and dust are swept back by the Sun's rays.

Comet

THE MOON is a ball of rock that orbits the Earth. All the planets, except for Mercury and Venus, have moons. Our Moon is a barren world pitted with craters. These have been blasted out by rocks called meteorites crashing down from space. There is no atmosphere on the Moon.

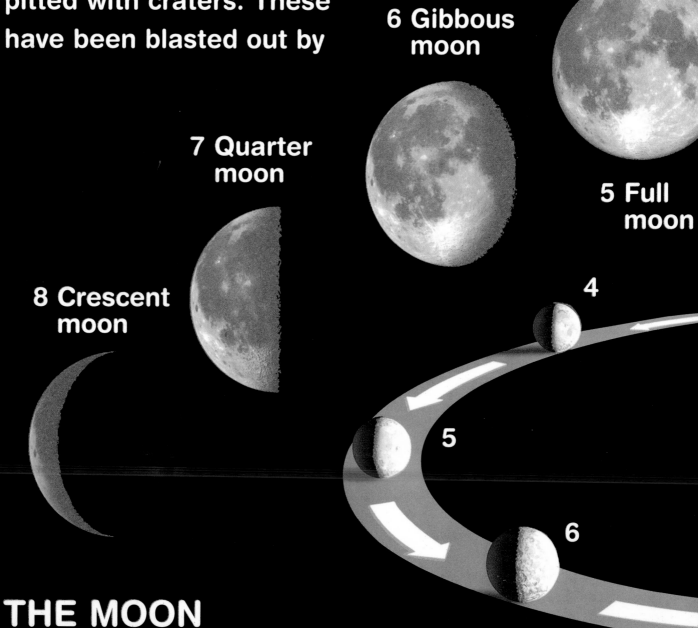

6 Gibbous moon

7 Quarter moon

5 Full moon

8 Crescent moon

4

5

6

THE MOON

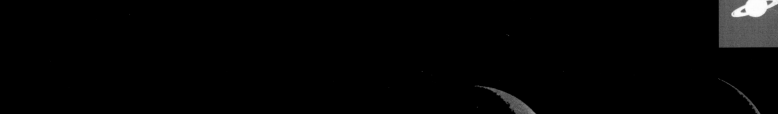

4 Gibbous moon

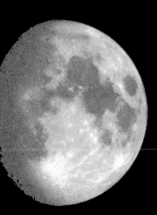

3 Quarter moon

2 Crescent moon

1 New moon

The shape of the Moon seems to change slightly each night *(above)* but it doesn't. The same side always faces us as the Moon orbits Earth *(below)*. It is our view of the sunlit part that changes.

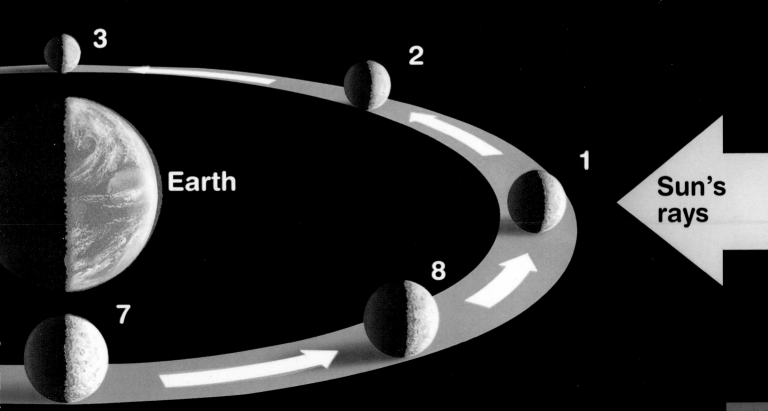

3

2

Earth

1

Sun's rays

8

7

Jupiter

Ganymede   Callisto

Io   Europa

JUPITER is large
enough to contain
1,300 Earths. Its patterns
of red, yellow, and white
are produced by high-
speed winds. The Great
Red Spot is a giant
storm. Jupiter's four
largest moons
(above right)
are called the
"Galileans."

SATURN is famous for
its rings. They are
made of billions of blocks
of ice and rock. Saturn's
largest moon, Titan, is
the only moon in the
solar system to have a
thick atmosphere.

Saturn

Titan

THE OUTER PLANETS

Triton

Uranus

Neptune

URANUS, the third largest planet, orbits the Sun lying almost on its side. The other planets orbit in a near-vertical position. Uranus has 11 faint rings and a family of 21 moons.

NEPTUNE is a bright blue globe with a few wispy clouds and, occasionally, dark spots. It has very faint rings. Neptune's largest moon, Triton, is the coldest world in the solar system.

PLUTO is the coldest, smallest, and most distant planet in the solar system. Its moon, Charon, is half its size.

Charon

Pluto

YEARS AGO, people saw patterns of stars in the night sky. They imagined their shapes to

CONSTELLATIONS

look like gods, heroes, or animals from legends. These star patterns are called constellations.

Being able to recognize constellations can help you find your way on a dark night.

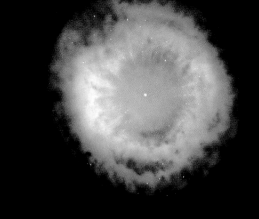

EVERYTHING that we know exists—stars, rocks, animals, people, air—belongs to the universe. Nearly all matter is contained in galaxies *(below)*.

The universe probably came into being about 15 billion years ago. There was a massive explosion called the big bang. All matter, energy, space—and time itself—were created in the big bang.

As the universe expanded, the first stars were formed. Many, like our Sun, will shine on for billions of years. But eventually they will swell into red giants before flaking away into space. A planetary nebula is all that will remain *(above)*. A massive star will grow into a supergiant before exploding in a supernova (the remains of one are pictured *below)*.

THE UNIVERSE

After a supernova, what is left of the old star may shrink to a tiny point. Around it, the force of gravity is so strong that nothing, not even light, can escape from it. We call these places black holes. Anything lying close to them, like the blue star shown in this illustration *(below),* will be dragged in!

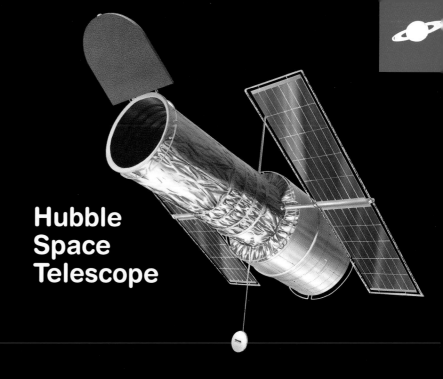

Hubble Space Telescope

Distances are so great in space that we have to use a special measure for them: a light-year. This is the distance that light, which moves at about 186,000 miles per second, travels in one year. Proxima Centauri, the nearest star to us (apart from the Sun), is 4.2 light-years away. The most distant objects we know are more than 13 billion light-years away!

ASTEROID A small rocky body that orbits the Sun.

BIG BANG The explosion in which the universe was created.

BLACK HOLE A region of space from which nothing, not even light, can escape.

COMET An lump of dust, ice and rock that orbits the Sun *(below)*. When it nears the Sun, long tails stream away from it.

CONSTELLATION A pattern of stars in the night sky.

CRATER A saucer-shaped feature found on the surface of some planets, moons and asteroids.

ECLIPSE The movement of a planet or moon in front of another, or in front of the Sun.

GALAXY An enormous cluster of stars, gas, dust, and planets *(far right)*.

GRAVITY The force that attracts all objects to each other. Gravity is the force that keeps the planets orbiting the Sun.

USEFUL WORDS

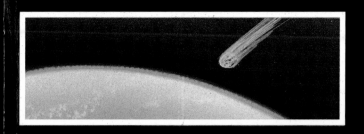

METEORITE A meteoroid that falls from space onto a planet or moon *(above).*

METEOROID A piece of rock or dust that hurtles through the solar system. When a meteoroid burns up close to Earth it is known as a **METEOR**.

ORBIT The circular or oval-shaped path followed by one object around another in space.

PLANET A world that orbits a star. It does not produce its own light.

SOLAR SYSTEM The Sun, the planets and their moons, comets, asteroids, meteoroids, dust, and gas.

STAR A globe of gas (eg. the Sun) that produces energy inside its core.

SUPERNOVA The massive explosion of a supergiant star.

UNIVERSE All matter and space.

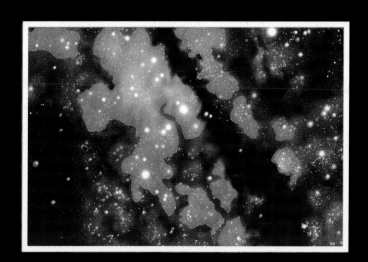

PLANET	DIAMETER	DAY measured in Earth days or hours	YEAR measured in Earth days or years	AVERAGE DISTANCE FROM SUN	SURFACE TEMPERATURE	MOONS
Mercury	3,031 miles	58.6 days	88 days	36 million miles	-274 to +662°F	none
Venus	7,521 miles	243 days	225 days	67 million miles	914°F	none
Earth	7,926 miles	23 hrs 56 min	365.26 days	93 million miles	-94 to +131°F	1
Mars	4,222 miles	24.6 hours	687 days	142 million miles	-215 to +79°F	2
Jupiter	88,788 miles	9.8 hours	11.8 years	484 million miles	-238°F	28
Saturn	74,901 miles	10.2 hours	29.4 years	887 million miles	-292°F	30
Uranus	31,765 miles	17.2 hours	84 years	1,783 million miles	-346°F	21
Neptune	31,404 miles	16.1 hours	164.8 years	2,794 million miles	-364°F	8
Pluto	1,444 miles	6.4 days	248 years	3,670 million miles	-364°F	1